Title Page

SOME UGLY THINGS THAT COULD BREAK DOWN YOUR BEAUTIFUL MARRIAGE,

(Know them to avoid them)

By

Counselor Adams Kittson-Kotsinya
(The Anti-Divorce Activist)
Outer Ring Road
Accra - Ghana

GPS Address: GA – 404 - 9307
Email: dontjustdivorce99@gmail.com
Tel: +233 548 330 021
+233 276 949 740

PREFACE

Do you know that you can purpose in your heart not to divorce or separate from your spouse, but if your spouse does not have the same mindset, you will divorce? Most divorces result from the couple not agreeing on many things during marriage.

Suppose you do not agree to keep your family together in rough and smooth times. In that case, you will surely divorce or damage your life, family joy, oneness, children, the beauty of marriage, and many other aspects of uniqueness to your marriage. Remember that divorce is the most disrespectful entity. It does not fear anyone; color and rank are nothing to it. The only thing it fears is you to have the knowledge and the desire not to give it room to operate in your marriage.

Many couples face different types of marital crises, including divorce, because they cannot read signs as and when divorce wants to strike their homes. Others, too, see the signs but ignore them, demonstrating a lack of knowledge. This is why I have written this points-to-point book to guide you through the walk of your marriage if you only listen to counsel not to divorce or separate, especially if you are a newly married couple.

It would be best not to divorce because divorce wastes a couple's time, money, and treasures and diminishes the value of your shared life and experiences.

If you do not have an idea to divorce, it is not enough to make you not divorce by the end of the day. The urgency of knowledge to fight your marital crises is essential. It is not just a tool but also a necessity.

If you are going through divorce too, I will urge you to take your time and consider the complicated things that come with divorce and how best you can solve your crisis before you finalize it.

This book is at the right time to help you conquer what may seem difficult about handling marital crises. Say no to with knowledge, not your vain mouth.

I hope you can be the right person to whom this book is available. Know the ugly things that could break down your marriage and avoid them by exercising daily obedience to what you have read. This excellent advice book will carry you through ugly times in your marriage.

I advise you to help your marriage, family, and children stay together in the test of time.

God bless you and always give you all the understanding you need in your marriage.

Contents

Chapter 1

SOME UGLY THINGS THAT COULD BREAK DOWN YOUR BEAUTIFUL MARRIAGE

1. Refusing to accept that everybody has some crises they are battling will make you leave your crises by divorce to go in for another crisis somewhere you know nothing about.

I want to tell you that seeing grown-up couples living happily together does not mean that they are perfectly okay with themselves or their crisis but that they have learned with time to ignore some of their weaknesses and challenges that could have broken down their beautiful marriages, some time ago. Why won't you know to be such a couple in your generation when crisis comes rather than divorce in times of marital turmoil?

2. Refusing always to learn to forgive in times of your marital crisis, especially when you think you must not forgive, will cause your divorce later. *Do you want that experience? There is some level of unforgiveness behind every divorce issue and some amount of repeated forgiveness behind every successful marriage you see in your community. So please make your choice now either to destroy your beautiful marriage in times of marital crisis or to build it up for life.*

3. Husband, do not maltreat your wife. That is, if you do not want your marriage to break down in the future, *Maltreatment will make your wife constantly frustrated,*

that will also make her not trust you at all, and that could be very dangerous to you with divorce in the future or on the next anniversary.

4. You will surely destroy the relationship you have with your husband if you are fond of secretly killing your husband with too much stress from every side of the marriage. *Married woman, please allow your husband to be at peace in his heart while with you; it will make him love you more, and divorce will be very far from your home.*

I will not be surprised if your husband one day desires to leave the marriage for you, and I know that will render you a divorcee. You would not be happy after that since women are primarily vulnerable when it comes to the consequences of divorce.

5. If you are deceived about the marital crisis, divorce, and remarriage, that could make you divorce within the shortest time in your marriage, especially closely or after ten years. *Many couples have divorced because they see other people divorcing here and there. The point is that divorce might look good in your eyes because of the bitterness you have in your heart towards your spouse.*

Still, it would be better to heal any bitterness, lest it kills both of you with some consequences you would not like to happen in the future, especially to your firstborn, who will, by all means, be vulnerable due to your divorce status.

6. Lack of money and too much of it can break down your marriage if you need to learn how to go about it in your daily life. *Many couples become involved in some way if some huge or little money comes into their hands. Instead of using their resources to heal the home and marriage, they instead use them to destroy the relationship they had with their spouse some time ago. Many wives also leave the marriage because their husbands do not have money to cater for them. Nevertheless, it is a shame to do that.*

Dear Wives, please, if your husbands cannot provide for you, do it as a single parent or wife, but in the marriage until a proper solution comes, then divorce since many women secretly take care of their husbands without knowing it yourself. Note that money can be one of the temptations for you to not have a successful marriage in the future.

7. Lack of communication on important issues can slowly or quickly dissolve your marriage during hot crises. So be careful always. *Most of the challenges I have witnessed in my career as an* ***Anti-Divorce Activist*** *are communication problems between couples. Dear couples, please try to talk about everything by first allowing your spouse to become your best friend and also someone you can always tolerate, no matter what the crisis might be presently or in the future. My dear husband or wife, in times of marital crisis, allow yourself to be talked to when the need arises rather than be arrogant due to*

the pain inside your heart against your spouse since it does not help an excellent marriage to continue.

8. Misunderstandings about your crisis and that of your spouse can destroy your marriage if you do not stop it soon. *Why misunderstand yourselves while you have now become one by marriage? Can one of your hands start to beat the other hand without a cause, or are you not mad yourself?*

Definitely No. Remember that misunderstanding is sometimes suitable for most marriages because you shall derive another understanding to keep the marriage going into other better anniversaries. Do not divorce your spouse because you do not get them on issues since it will surely be a sign that you do not also have understanding yourself for all this while.

9. Lack of love from your side as a husband can cause the marriage to be broken down. *Remember that all marital crises can be rectified with love between you and your wife. Remember also that if love can make a man fly without wings, how much more can he forgive his spouse for a beautiful marriage to continue again?*

10. If the lack of love from a husband's side can destroy a beautiful marriage, then the lack of submission from your side as a wife can soon destroy the same beautiful marriage. *It would help if you were very careful to render submission to your*

husband rather than to your bosses and pastors, especially in times of marital crisis since in lack of submission, most divorce schemes are hidden.

I believe you must reserve some submission for your husband. If any situation arises between you and him, you can consider him since submission is easily quenched in times of marital crisis. Be a unique wife; it does not make you look like a fool but rather like someone who values her marriage.

11. Being irresponsible as a couple will surely stand still in your marriage. *If both of you are irresponsible, the marriage cannot stand since all successful marriages can only be based on accountability. To me, I see marriage to*

be in a ratio that should be shared in husband 50 and wife 50 or 40:60, which can either be the husband or the wife, husband ten and wife90, and 30:70. You have to be responsible for something to lessen the burden on your other spouse if he or she is complaining, lest divorce strikes later.

Marriage does not need one spouse to be lazy since money, which is the basis of all responsibilities, is required occasionally. Some couples are okay if their spouses do not contribute anything to the welfare of the marriage. However, the fact is, those couples who feel they are not contributing anything good to the marriage are still contributing something insignificant but helpful that the other spouse cannot identify unless that spouse is no longer in the marriage by divorce or separation.

12. Lack of children has destroyed many marriages, and yours could be one of its victims if you are fond of chasing your desire to have wonderful children with your spouse when the opportunity is also not there. *Let me ask you, what will you do if a good doctor tells you that your wife will instantly die if she attempts to give birth to her first child?*

Will you still force her to go to the maternity ward to have a child or children from that same wife of yours? If Not, you must take it easy if children have not yet come into your marriage since your spouse is more important than the children you want, and your wife is the one who will give you the children you need in your marriage.

13. Too many children can cause a divorce or even a separation. *If you do not regulate the number of your children, your spouse will see it as a burden, making them give up easily by divorce. If your husband wants two or three children, try to give those exact numbers lest he blames you for the hardship in the family since taking care of children is very burdensome when the finances are not there.*

14. Unfaithfulness on both sides can also damage your home and marriage if you do not learn to be a faithful husband or wife after reading this point. *A mistake of sleeping with another person will make your spouse lose their trust in you, and that could make your spouse let go of the marriage unless God intervenes. You are so forced to be faithful to your spouse*

because of the predator called divorce. Do not desire another man or woman apart from your spouse, though the temptations and the opportunities might come from time to time as you journey the long journey of marriage.

15. Another ugly thing that can make you put away your husband or wife quickly is when you directly listen to your family members to divorce your spouse in times of ugly marital crisis. *Remember that family members are most pretenders, making themselves feel as if they are enjoying the best marriage ever with their spouses. Note that they also have the same marital crisis just like yours, or maybe theirs are even worse than yours, so do not be envious of them to destroy yours, especially if it is your father or mother influencing you to divorce your husband*

or wife you are having a problem with today. ***Allow God to speak to you in those times rather than them.***

16. Wickedly and secretly marrying another person without the knowledge of your present spouse will make you lose your original and covenant husband or wife, which God has documented in heaven. *Seeking for greener pastures somewhere deceives many people.*

For that reason, men and women marry another person secretly to be in another better state or stage of life. However, do not you think treating your spouse in that manner is total wickedness since you know your spouse has trusted you with their entire life regarding marriage? If you can treat your spouse so wickedly, do not blame them if they curse you with all the curses of this world because you have been a hard-minded spouse in your generation, leading to divorce.

17. Hardship or extreme poverty can also destroy your marriage just as too much riches can gravely destroy your beautiful marriage, as I said earlier. *Therefore, it will be better to make the home or the marriage very comfortable for you to bear since the hardest thing to bear on this earth is to have extreme poverty in your life, and that of your marriage, too.*

Husband, do not be too spiritually or financially poor; work harder to make some income for your family to survive. Moreover, my dear wife, do not support or accept the poverty state of your husband;

help him excel in liberating the family from poverty. Beloved husband, you have to know that where there is some hardship, it simply means that the husband is not working or is stupidly lazy.

18. Separations between you can often destroy your *healthy-looking* marriage, especially if you love practicing them. *A crisis will tempt you to go to your family house for a crisis rest or break, but remember that marriage does not need any form of separation to succeed. So, be in balance as to when to separate when any crisis consumes you both. You have to remember that your marital separation can lead you to other dangerous challenges like adultery. In addition, do you want to be called an adulterous woman while married?*

19. Another ugly thing that can destroy your marriage, which you need to be careful about, is the bad or good reasons you used for marrying your husband or wife in the first place. *All that I know is that the reasons people use for marriage are many, and each can put a good relationship in long-lasting silence. So, my dear friend, what reason did you use to marry your spouse in the first place, and what will come of you if those reasons you have did not come through as you expected? So check your reasons for marriage because it could be the stepping stone on which your marriage can be destroyed in the future.*

20. Marrying your affluent spouse to be more decadent or rich in the future is a

lousy reason for marriage. It will, by all means, destroy your marriage in the future since it is possibly assured that most people cannot always be prosperous until the end of time since some rich have wings that can fly away, as the bible says. Also, some people are very careless when they encounter riches in their lifetime. *You must know that riches have reasons and seasons that come into one's life. Suppose you cannot identify those reasons and seasons for them coming to you.*

In that case, you shall divorce for those same reasons and in seasons of lacking those riches too, maybe on your 26th anniversary, after that, or even before the 26th anniversary. Will you leave or divorce your once-upon-a-time affluent spouse because they are now poor?

21. Were you married to be pregnant for your husband or because you are already pregnant and, for that matter, your husband wants to marry you based on that? *Do not be too happy because one thing I know is that the success of marriage cannot only be on the availability of children or pregnancy, for many have gotten divorced, yet they have their choices in pregnancy. At the same time, others, too, have been disappointed with divorce because the pregnancy they were looking for has not yet come their way.*

22. Marrying for physical appearance reasons, like your spouse's having

beautiful eyes, nose, lips, and even physical stature, can disappoint you one day, which will lead you to your divorce status since the world is engulfed with surprises, issues, and changes. *Therefore, if I were you, I would focus more on the inner abilities of my spouse than the physical appearance since most couples are only interested in the physical stature of their spouses, which is also leading most of them into the state of divorce.*

23. Marrying your spouse because they presently have a good job or salary will tempt you to let go of your spouse by divorce if the state of unemployment comes around the marriage in the future. *I am not saying you should marry a spouse who is not working; I am saying that you must be able to stand if things change to*

the negative, either for a long or a short time. If you divorce your spouse in times when he or she is not working, it could be one of the most devastating things you could have ever done against your husband or wife. If you have the mindset of leaving your spouse due to a lack of salary or job, you shall then be divorcing one spouse to another because people cannot always work as you think. In life, there will, by all means, be a break time and continuation time as far as marriage is concerned.

24. Marrying to be famous in the future because your spouse is already famous will disappoint you later because most people who are famous spouses are not known like them. *What will your marital status be if your spouse decides to hide*

you from the public for their purposes or your safety's sake without knowing your spouse's intentions? Please, whether your spouse is famous or not, try to be the good husband or wife you must be for the marriage to succeed. Remember that being famous is for a while, but marriage is for life if you decide not to divorce your spouse sooner or later.

25. Marrying to have children and, after that, deciding to leave the marriage if a crisis comes up will indeed render you a divorcee since you do not know what the future holds as far as there are unfortunates in life too. *I wonder if most couples marry to have children, and after they have gotten the children, they start to create various marital crises for the marriage to break down, and after that,*

they take the children and go their ways with them.

What sort of ugly intention is that? Is marriage and family life not made to be lived with two learned people and not only one person? Trust me, if you make your children be abandoned by their mother or father, you shall also be abandoned later when you can no longer take the responsibilities that come with your children's welfare.

Do you want to be called a single dad or mum? Remember that it is an ugly experience and not remarkable to be talked about in any field since it is a wrong standard to God's plans concerning how families and marriages should go about in this world.

26. You think you cannot stand the opposing sides of your spouse when they come, and it will surely make you leave the marriage soon as life and marriage are made up of good and bad moments. *Are you planning to leave the marriage because you do not like how your spouse misbehaves nowadays?*

Indeed, you are not happy about that, but remember that that is the very moment your spouse also really needs you than ever, though their character will not show it. Many couples are dying young in the time that they must not die because their life companions are nowhere to be found around the marriage in times of those crises.

27. If you are in the marriage only for the good side of it, then it is an ugly intention since life is not programmed to be only good but bad as well. *Dear husband and wife, are you loving your spouse because they have been good to you all this while? If your answer is yes, what will be the stand about your marriage if time or the table changes to what you do not like about your spouse on the next anniversary?*

28. If you are fond of thinking that you are not compatible as a couple to be together for the years ahead, you both will bring divorce before your tenth anniversary; trust *me on this. Remember that you are not computer accessories but human beings who can iron out delicate issues even if they seem harsh. It is mouth used*

to solve marital problems, and two hearts used to incline understanding concerning marriage crisis.

Therefore, you can be compatible from now on if you are tempted to say in your heart that you are not compatible with continuing the marriage, especially in times of marital crisis. The issues related to incompatibility in most couples are based on the couples being irresponsible about solving their marital turmoil from time to time as they see them coming.

29. Deciding not to like or love to suffer for a long or a short time in your marriage, especially in times of marital crisis, will make you divorce your spouse on a foolish note. *Some sufferings in the marriage can come in the form of*

sickness, unemployment, loss, poverty, anxiety, frustration, and the desire to abandon the marriage for another spouse.

Therefore, if you have not prepared enough to suffer to resolve your spouse's shortcomings, you shall run away before the best solution comes to your spouse. If you do not want to suffer with your spouse in the future, then you can never be a good husband or wife. It is also a sign that you are one of the cruelest husbands or wives by all standards in your generation, and no one needs to remarry you because that wickedness is still in your blood, which you can unleash on your next spouse.

30. You allow your parents to interfere in your marriage and personal affairs. *You can decide to take advice, but not as and*

when they are advising you to leave your marriage for another person to occupy because you are having some marital crisis.

31. Changing to the opposing sides of life when your husband or wife strictly dislikes it will also destroy your marriage, even if you do not want it to be broken. *I know some negative life comes unknowingly to us, and some also come by situations, but you must fight harder to be positive with God's power and with self-consciousness since you do not know the type of spouse you got married to unless crisis begins to come.*

Many couples plan to put away their spouses because of their negative lives, but the good ones plan to save their marriages, though they also have some shortcomings. It is always good to try to be the excellent couple that you are in times of marital crisis, and that is the very secret of saving your beautiful marriage when the crisis arrives on any anniversary.

32. Not agreeing with your spouse on most essential family issues and that of the marriage can also trigger divorce and separations later. You must be conscious about not dragging issues for long with your spouse since we have different temperaments. *In marriage, it is reasonable and wiser to compromise most times on problems, whether you are the wife or the husband, but do not compromise to do evil in the future, correct your spouse if he or she is tempted*

to commit a crime because it will also affect you later if the law is catching him or her.

33. Allowing foolish pride to lead you as a husband will make you throw away your wife; before you realize it, it will be too late. *Being proud is foolishness since failure follows it, and you are not going to send all that you are pleased about to the grave or to gain a successful marriage on this earth.*

34. Allowing foolishness to lead you as a wife will easily tempt your husband to think he made the wrong choice about marriage. *So be wise as a wife like Abigail, Sarah, Elizabeth, Esther, and many other incredible women in the Bible. Your husband will be proud of you later,*

especially in times of marital crisis. In times of marital crisis, do not talk or complain too much since it will usually make you get the wrong solutions from those you are complaining to.

35. Just listening to anything nonsense or any information that comes your way as a husband or a wife can destroy your marriage in the future, so beware always about people who bring you both good and bad information. *One day a particular wife had an infection in her vagina. She went to the hospital, and what the doctor directly said was that the infection was coming from the husband.*

The wife quickly asked the doctor if that could mean her husband had been unfaithful to her in any way. In addition, the doctor replied, 'Yes,' and continued, "Go and ask him." The woman went home in a mood of anger and started accusing the husband and calling him all manner of names because the infection was severe to her. That was the beginning of their marital crisis, and another person advised her to see another doctor; when she went, the other doctor told her that she got that infection on the toilet and that she should stop going to a public bathroom and she was administered some medicines and the infection was cured. However, by then, the husband had already left the house.

So you see, just listening to anything can destroy your beautiful home, and it will be too late for you since one of you will be hurt when you are accused wrongly. ***I advise, "Do not always believe the first***

information that comes to you if only you want to save your home and family from divorce and separation."

36. Allowing yourself to be deceived by another unmarried woman to fulfill her sexual desires because of the little money she has will surely make you leave your wonderful wife one day for her. She will start to maltreat you later because she surely knows that you came to her because of the money she showed to you some time ago, and that will leave you in a state of regret for many years.

I have identified this as the one thing most husbands who have divorced before become stupid in the later part of their marital lives because they know or understand that all the women or wives in town are the same. Be wise not to divorce if you are tempted.

37. Allowing yourself to be deceived by another man his wife is tormenting in his house can make you pity such a man for falling into sin, not in love with such a man, since it could be that you are also facing some challenges in your marriage with your husband. Still, the truth is that action or sin will lead to divorce, and you shall regret it later.

The fact is you are an unwise wife to secretly allow yourself to be slept with by another married man somewhere since all signs show that you are just a sex tool to that man since he is still keeping his dirty wife in his house without divorcing her to bring you in. If you are in this state, I advise you to quit that secret relationship before it comes out one day since you know that all things will come to light one day.

38. I am talking about things that can destroy your beautiful marriage so that you can be careful about them. One of those ugly things is that you are not achieving your personal goals in life and that of your spouse. *That can become a severe marital crisis that can lead to divorce in the future. For example, suppose you do not become the man of God, the doctor, the lawyer, or the businesswoman your spouse was looking for in you before the marriage began.*

In that case, it can be devastating if your spouse does not change their focus on becoming what they desired you to be in the first place. Dear couples, note that if you did not become what you wanted, forget about it and focus on the things available to keep the marriage going. Since not everything must come to pass, remember that even in the Bible, not all prophesies have been accomplished, but some are yet to come. So be calm on your spouse to save the marriage in times of marital crisis.

39. Your children being preferred over the husband or the wife can also destroy a beautiful and potential marriage. *That is also a quick route to divorce. Still, it usually happens after the marriage has taken its tenth to twentieth anniversary when one child is preferred over the other children, leading to jealousy, bitterness,*

and later divorce because one party is unhappy. It will be wiser to periodically do some family meetings with your children to iron out essential issues, lest your absence after your death will be something you would not like in your grave.

Do not just leave your children to their fates while you are alive; instead, talk to them because it can iron out the hidden issues that can finally lead to divorce or even save the marriage.

40. Disvaluing your spouse because you are just angry with yourself or with your spouse will make you not continue the marriage again. *Mostly, it is a marital crisis that makes you not see your spouse as a person who is essential in the*

marriage. That is why it is always good to deal with your situation from time to time as they come and vow not to abandon your partner, lest unhappiness will be your portion in the time that you must not be unhappy in life.

41. I have written a lot about anger in one of my books, but the little I can say here is that extreme anger could be one of the main stands of your divorce status if you do not control it as it comes. *Remember that anger is not a respecter of persons; for that matter, anybody can be angry and cause damage because of that same anger. Beware of your anger constantly. Note that anger can make you kill your spouse either secretly or openly, and you will regret it later because anger has a time to come and a time to go.*

42. A fit of uncontrolled anger leading to un-forgiveness, long-harbored anger that can take more than two years in your heart, can finally destroy your beautiful marriage in the next year. *So avoid this one, too. If your spouse offends you, learn to take it away from your heart within six hours. It won't be easy sometimes, but it will be worth it doing that to avoid divorce coming your way as a husband or a wife.*

43. Suspiciousness, which is always having dishonest thoughts or lifestyles about your husband or wife, will make your spouse uncomfortable with you.

44. Rumors could also destroy your marriage, so be careful of those who feed you with messages about your spouse in

their presence or absence. *Anyone who believes a rumor is not wise enough to be a husband or a wife in the first place since most rumors are not true themselves or they only have a little amount of truth in them, which is not worth destroying your marriage for them.*

45. Turning to an alcoholic husband or wife along the journey of the marriage can surely stagnate the relationship you have with your spouse or can even generate divorce or separation without remedies. *You have to remember that drunkards typically smell wrong a lot, and maybe your spouse would not love your drinking body odor, and that could lead to divorce if your spouse is not just wise like you. So, avoid alcohol totally and do not follow vain fun since those who follow the*

fun of this life become poor by the end of the day, and that could also lead to divorce in the latter part of your life.

46. Hidden past life like committed abortions, which have rendered you the woman barren while your husband or wife also wants children, will make your husband search for children outside the marriage, and that could bring divorce later since the other woman will possess your husband with the children that she has with your husband.

You would not be happy, as you know that husbands love children because that is their glory, just as your glory, too, is to marry as a woman. *Remember that it would be far better to marry with a pregnancy than to commit an abortion before your marriage day since it might cost you your life happiness concerning children bearing. Most Christians are fond of committing dangerous abortions even if their marriage is in the next three months.*

47. Committing common mistakes in your marriage might force your husband or wife to leave you suddenly and sadly.

48. Another thing that could destroy your marriage is repeated mistakes. Some couples are adamant about following instructions from their spouses; that is, they will constantly do things they have been told not to do, and sadly, those people are divorced, too, without any callback because their spouses are tired of them.

I know you are a human being with faults, but you must remember that repeated mistakes could destroy you, your spouse's life, your children, and future generations. So, why commit many errors in your life, especially in your marriage, to hurt your spouse's feelings, leading to a long-lasting divorce? It is not correct. Please reduce the mistakes you are aware of in your marriage and those you are told to by your spouse.

49. Unnecessary arguments, too, can also damage your marriage. You must stop it if you are fond of unnecessarily debating essential and unimportant issues in your marriage, especially between you and the wife. *Please, couples, cease to argue about things if that argument will bring*

divorce later since many people do not want to say due to their evil egos. Do you contend with your spouse, please? It is hazardous if you do not know how to control it, or it will end your marriage. Due to unnecessary arguments, many couples think they are incompatible couples who can stay until the end.

50. Being a cruel husband or wife when you know your spouse is weak or down can make your spouse leave the marriage since no one wants to be with a wicked husband or a wife. *Please, if you are a good husband or wife today, you should not turn to be cruel in the future because divorce might be hiding there unknowingly to you, and it will hurt me that you will divorce in the future since*

you did not plan to divorce in the future from the start of your marriage.

51. You need to be more supportive as a husband or even helpful to your wife, which will confuse her about the marriage since she might be looking into other people's helping spouses' marriages without you knowing it, which could make her compare you to other husbands. So, help your wife sometimes with the chores since doing that is even more beautiful.

Remember that the second husband who will remarry your wife will do that a hundred times to keep your unwise wife who will love to divorce you because you do not support her in her endeavors. So, if you learn to support your wife in the kitchen four times a week, it will not kill you, dear husband; it will help grow your marital friendship.

52. As a husband, allowing your mistresses (girlfriends) to come and disturb your wife in your house will make her mistrust you.

53. Losing the cord of your friendship will one way or generate divorce with time since most beautiful marriages are on cords of friendship, not just a friendship but a friendship like *David* and *Jonathan's* type of friendship. *If you have lost the cord of your friendship as a couple, try to rebind it once again since it is typical for some friendships to break down sometimes. That is why David and Jonathan constantly renewed their*

friendship; they knew they would wax cold since there was a constant separation between them. Remember that you are in a marriage, and your marriage must not easily be broken down like others did in times of marital crisis.

54. Loving your other friends more than your husband or wife will also break your marriage if only your spouse wants the same friendship you give your friends. *I know some friends were there before your spouse came into marriage with you, but do you not remember that your spouse, too, left some important people for your sake? It is your turn to do that for your spouse. Please remember to make your spouse your best friend, and your marriage will be excellent in the view of*

others without them knowing the type of crisis you have as a couple.

55. Still womanizing as a husband but yet married to a wonderful wife who gives you all that you could want from a woman will make that same wife of yours run away from the marriage because she will see you as a husband who is not content in life. *Dear man, I believe sexual satisfaction is all about releasing your sperm into the vagina of a woman, and your wife is purposely there for you?*

If our wives are not enough for us now, then we are mad people as husbands, and we will be lonely later in our lives if we divorce or if our second wives understand the truth that they are not our proper wives. I believe many people marry second husbands or wives because they do not know that it is a sin, but one day, true light about divorce will come to them, and they will abandon us. Be careful when marrying a divorcee, or do not marry them.

56. Still prostituting but yet married to a husband who is doing his best to please you will make him put you away soon since he has the biblical standards to divorce you if you commit adultery one day in the course of the marriage. *You will be quickly divorced if you are still keeping your ex-boyfriend, so be content to appreciate the penis of your husband, and the best will come out of it. Do you know it is a shame to be sleeping with a man who did not put the wedding ring on your*

finger because you are not happy in your marriage?

Any other man who sleeps with you while you are a married woman sees you as a pure, foolish woman without you knowing it yourself, and he will not love to marry you after you have finally divorced your husband unless he is also a silly person like you or not having self-consciousness.

There are a lot of those bad guys who sleep with people's wives in town; they do not have God's principles in them. Avoid them now as a wife and note that they come in the sweeter ways.

57. Selfishness, which is always fighting for yours only, will make your spouse feel left alone, and they will also feel

rejected. *You are married, so if you buy clothes for yourself, try to buy some for your spouse too. Another example of selfishness is secretly building your house, moving in alone, and getting the full license to play your harlot acts there. However, you have had a fantastic wife from the beginning of the marriage. It shall not be well with you if you hurt your spouse's feelings with divorce or separation.*

58. Any imprisonment can also destroy your beautiful and growing marriage. The fact is that both long and short imprisonment can ruin your marriage, depending on the type of husband or wife you get married to. *So why not be careful in your doings with people all around you since some severe imprisonment is*

equally like divorce? Ask yourself whether your husband or wife will wait for you if you are jailed for thirty-five years for a crime you committed or the one you are suspected of. When it happens like that, you will force your husband or wife to commit adultery in the future against him or herself since most spouses cannot genuinely stay without sex and companionship, and you know that. Stay clean always from bad friends and bad businesses as a husband or a wife to save the marriage simply because your marriage needs your constant presence to succeed.

59. Voluntary or involuntary cheating on your spouse could immediately destroy your marriage, and you need to be careful about that from time to time when the

temptations and opportunities come around your environment as a husband or a wife. *The sad thing is that some couples cheat for the first time, and they are caught and immediately they are divorced without any explanation. Since you do not know your spouse that much, why try to cheat on your spouse when you know they will go away from the marriage, and you will be left alone to suffer in adultery, uncleanliness, or even loneliness?*

60. You still admire your ex-girl or boyfriend, and due to that, you keep on texting yourselves secretly, which will slowly destroy your marriage and home with time since secretly texting another romantic person is another form of fornication, depending on the things that you text yourselves with.

I know those **secrets** *are not always accurate because one day, those* **secrets** *could be the ground for an intense divorce against your wish. You will regret it later, especially if you do not get anybody else to marry you again after your husband or wife has divorced you. My advice is if your former woman or person sends you HI on what app or on messenger, reply not to save the marriage because your marriage is worth more than that relationship you will be going into with your former to destroy your home and life finally.*

61. Selling hard drugs, dealing with illegal drugs, or taking drugs yourself will destroy your beautiful home one day, primarily if your spouse does not support

your evil ways. *Remember that many couples have secretly exposed themselves to the drugs that they do, and they are now in long-term jail. Do you know your spouse enough? Remember that most drug dealers end up in the prison yards, and you could be one of them. Your marriage, too, will be broken due to that, and you will later say, 'Had I known,' but it will always be too late for you and me. So, stop doing drugs if you are into one to save your children, wife, yourself, and your marriage.*

62. An anti-church wife or husband could intrigue divorce on a fast note. *Most couples think that it is a crime to marry an anti-church person, so for that reason, they divorce their anti-church spouses to go in for the church type, but they forget*

that the divorce rate is somewhat higher among those who go to church and those who call themselves Christians.

Suppose Christians and non-Christians have the same common marital crisis. Why, then, would I force myself to purposely marry a Christian, not knowing the type of crisis she might carry along to the marriage, which will trigger divorce later?

63. Not being the communicable type to your husband or wife will make your spouse stay longer at night in town with the communicable types, and slowly by slowly, his or her desires will become cold towards you, which will bring divorce later. *Do you know that your husband or wife can divorce you just because you do*

not like talking or commenting on issues concerning you or other things in the marriage? So I think you must learn sometimes to be what you think you are not because of marriage since marriage is the center of learning, as I said earlier in some of my books.

64. Valuing your siblings more than your spouse can damage your home and your spouse's feelings; divorce will follow up later. *Sometimes, to get solutions to your marital crisis, you must put yourself in your spouse's shoes. How would you feel if your wife listened to his brothers more than you, just as you are fond of listening to your sisters more than your wife? Try to use the golden rule in your marriage sometimes, 'which is to do to others what*

you want others to do for you, and divorce will run away forever.

65. Being open enough to your spouse in all things could bring divorce later. *Do not be fond of hiding things in the marriage since you are not in the marriage with yourself only but with another person, even if you are the husband. So tell your spouse your hidden buildings, lands, children, or child and bank accounts since later exposure of them could make an unwise husband or a wife leave the marriage just for those excuses sakes.*

66. Do you know that not training yourself to enjoy your wife's only food can lead to many ugly things that could destroy your marriage later in life? *If you do not want your wife's food, another woman's food*

will be pleasant to you, leading to other temptations that will destroy your marriage. Dear husband, if you say your wife does not know how to cook so well and, for that matter, you will not eat her food, remember that even with professional food vendors, not all of them know how to cook. So, it would be better to make her learn more about cooking than to divorce your wife just because of an unwell-known cooked food.

67. Lack of sex can destroy your beautiful marriage. *As far as marriage shortcomings are concerned, by all means, one of your sexual feelings will gradually go cold one day. You need to be conscious of not using that to destroy the marriage, and it can even start just after a few years in the marriage. If you think*

marriage is only based on constant sexual activities, you shall surely divorce, to your surprise, in a short time.

So, give yourself to your spouse most often since that could be the main reason you are in the marriage today with your spouse, and maybe there are other reasons too, I do not know. So, do not ever deny sex any time it is being asked of you since you may not know your spouse's feelings level at that very moment whether you like it or not.

68. Too much sexual activity can destroy your beautiful marriage. *You have to know that too much of everything is terrible, and we defy our upbringing, so you must be balanced if the criticism is going too high about your love of sex. If*

you think you are too addicted to sex, then please learn how to tame yourself just as I did some time ago to save the marriage from divorce since maybe your spouse has not gotten the exact knowledge about sex and marriage and how to get adjusted to it for the marriage not to break down upon that.

69. Secretly stealing from your husband or wife will surely destroy your marriage with time. *Most of us are not fortunate enough to marry a spouse other than a thief, but that does not mean we should divorce them because some of our stealing spouses can change to be positive one day if the necessary solutions are found. The first and last person you should not steal from is your husband or wife since you can ask whatever you want, and you shall*

be given in the smallest or the most significant way than to steal.

Your husband or wife will entirely be disappointed in you if he or she finds you stealing from his or her secret secrets. But be warned that I feel bothered when you are stolen from me; you must also learn how to give to your spouse since most couples steal due to their necessities. Do not be headstrong on your husband or wife, lest stealing be a secret, and its exposure might trigger divorce one day, to our surprise. It would help if you also had a spouse who wanted to divorce because of a stealing nature.

70. Simply being a foolish husband or wife will surely make your spouse leave the marriage one day since all human

beings hate to see or to be with foolish partners. *One sign of being a foolish husband or wife is when you are evil in all your doings, especially with the person you always sleep with or have children. If you are irrational in all your endeavors, you will also and surely tempt your spouse to become foolish like you.*

If your spouse also lacks marital self-consciousness or simply, your foolishness as a husband or a wife will make you go away from the marriage one day yourself when you must not leave the marriage. I have noticed that foolish cases are the majority causes of most divorces in town today. Therefore, anytime you want to divorce your spouse, check whether foolishness is not leading you, and the best way to know that is to ask someone's advice on your decision to put away your spouse due to a crisis.

71. Another thing that can destroy your marriage is when you *esteem* your dog (pet(s)) more than your wife. *I wonder if most husbands esteem their dogs or cats more than their wives. I know that those who love animals or dogs are dogs or animals themselves since they are dogs or animals that play with their fellow dogs or animals.*

Most men in my community esteem their pets more than their wives. What a pity! The sad truth is that if you esteem animals more than people, especially your wife, it equally makes you an animal yourself. Remember that animals will give you no help and cannot be more dangerous than humans.

It might be nothing to you, but I know what I am talking about as I have been an Anti-Divorce activist for some time now; I know what is destroying beautiful marriages, and I tell you the truth that most lovers of dogs are destroying their beautiful marriages, which must not be so.

72. Taking advantage of your spouse's personality because you know that the same spouse of yours is undoubtedly loving you are taking advantage of will destroy your marriage soon. Your spouse will lose hope in you one day, and divorce will surely follow up if you do not change from being irritating to your spouse.

If you are fond of hurting your spouse because of the availability of your spouse's love, note that your spouse will be wise one day. You shall lose your beautiful husband or wife to another person, and that will hurt you for many years to come. So always be genuine with your spouse and respect them for what they are for life since that keeps good marriages long.

73. Another thing that can destroy your marriage is taking advantage of your spouse because you think your spouse cannot survive without you. That mindset will disappoint you one day, and it will undoubtedly lead to divorce or separation. *Your home or marriage will be broken soon, and you shall face four other stages of divorce, to your surprise, because there*

is foolishness in your heart depending on how you negatively turn up to your spouse in times of his or her needs.

Please do not take advantage of your spouse because he or she is poor; defend less, weak, not having a defending spirit or not having a firm family name, maybe unemployed, most friendly or unfriendly because he or she is a good wife or a husband. Some couples even take advantage of their spouses because their spouse is the playing type or one who wants the marriage to stand against all the odds of the crisis, etc.

My dear couples, do not be meaningless to your spouse, which will lead to your divorce, and do not also turn to be cleaver after your marriage has been broken since it is also meaningless.

74. Playing with the particular person who has devoted him or herself to be with you for life will surely break the marriage. *Many people lose the special people in their lives before they know how special those people are. It would help if you were not such at all. If your spouse has said or vowed to be with you for life, please honor them, and you shall save the marriage with that same attitude you have inside you.*

75. Can illiteracy be one of the ugly things that can destroy a beautiful marriage? Yes, it can. *Since many marital crises' solutions come through reading, if you do not know how to read or listen to people*

read, you shall indeed be divorcing soon since you are not learning anything from something. Note that many illiterates' marriages have been broken down compared to those who know how to read something since knowledge is compelling when you have one.

How can you gain massive knowledge from this book if you do not know how to read it? It means you would be lost, and you will be lost until you start reading something from my marital books. Thank God if you are reading this book.

76. If you do not tend to take any advice when given in times of your marital crisis, you will end your marriage at the same time you decide not to listen to advice of any sort. *Divorce awaits you in the next*

month or year if you have this attitude of not listening to wise people if they talk about divorce and its consequences to you.

I pray that no one marries you after you have been divorced or that you should get another worse person than your former spouse because you are very stubborn; there and then, you will understand why I am saying that you should be careful about the ugly things that can destroy a beautiful marriage like yours.

77. Not being able to identify or accept the fates that come with your marriage or spouse can also root out divorce or separation within the shortest time of your marriage. *Some fates can come in the form that you must break into separation before*

the marriage takes another prosperous level; others, too, you have to divorce yourself at the court to be called back to be joined back into another Holy matrimony. I think that is why the Bible says we should not remarry if we divorce so that we can be reconciled back to our God-given spouse.

The turn of fate will surely return if you do not have any other spouse in your heart to go in for after you have divorced your once-loved spouse, but some couples rush into another marriage with another unknown crisis, which could be higher than the first one. Suppose you do not identify your fate about your marriage and accept it.

In that case, you shall surely divorce and divorce again since anyone you will tend to marry someday to come after you have divorced has some manner of fate issues to battle with either now or in the future.

78. Often, cases with the laws of the land that you live in will push divorce out soon. *Many couples want a successful marriage but always struggle with people in higher positions. It will make you unhappy with your marriage or even your dear spouse. So be careful when taking the loans as a husband or a wife since the loans can make you sad in the middle part of your marriage, though in the beginning, you were happy.*

Be careful to do a clean business with people around you, as I said earlier, since because of some human cases, many wonderful husbands and wives are in prison or the unseen world and it is making the other spouse commit various sins against God, which is contrary to the demands of a clean or Christian marriage.

79. Impregnating another woman apart from your wife can destroy your marriage if your wife does not get the right counselor to advise her urgently. *Please note that mistakenly impregnating another woman will push your wife to the wall to put you away since she cannot stand the heat of the jealousy that comes with you having another woman.*

Do you want that to happen to you, or do you think you do not care? If you do not care, I pray that your next woman be worse than your first wife; there, you shall care because you shall be frustrated for many years until you reconcile.

80. I wonder why most of my colleague pastors are being divorced here and there by their wives; this happens because the pastor husbands are fond of valuing their church members more than their very wives, which usually puts their wives in competition with them. It will be wiser to esteem your wife and avoid divorce as a man, God. Jesus did not say that we should put away our wives to keep Him the CHRIST. If putting away your wife for CHRIST could be the point of your mind, why did the same CHRIST say that He hates divorce?

If you divorce your husband or wife, you have committed a sin that cannot easily be forgiven unless you reconsider a careful reconciliation no matter how many years you have been divorced, and note that no divorcee will enter into the kingdom of heaven just as any other sin.

If all divorcees will go to heaven by the end of the day just by asking for forgiveness of sin, then what are we doing with our wives or waiting for since we did not also marry the best wives we wanted to marry in the first place? Do not be deceived into separating from your spouse just because of another man or woman somewhere; it shows you know little about what could destroy your beautiful marriage.

81. Another thing that can destroy your marriage is when you respect money more than your husband or wife. *Some of us will travel far to search for money to cater to the family but forget that a family needs two couples to make it a success with the little they can be contented with. If one couple is better, God could not have given Adam Eve. Think about that, my dear reader. Do not travel to the United States of America or other places for ten years and above and reject your wife or husband since silently, it will make your spouse go in for another person, and it will bring many problems in the future if you still love yourself. However, you have remarried to other couples due to your ugly condition.*

Your marriage status should prevent you from traveling just like that, as you know your spouse might need you most at times without you knowing it. How would you feel if your spouse remarries because you have stayed too long while traveling, considering your spouse is flesh and blood with hot feelings?

82. Abandonment of one spouse or the other has destroyed many marriages, and you could be a victim, too, if you also unexpectedly abandon your sweet spouse due to a condition beyond them. *If your spouse feels you have abandoned them when they needed you most, divorce can follow up since you have one cord of marriage ethics. In a divorce story I witnessed, the husband tried calling the*

wife on the phone several times because a team of police caught him up.

He only wanted the wife to confirm that he was on his way to the house due to the ugly time the police caught him, but the wife refused to pick up the phone because there was quarreling between them in the morning. The man felt abandoned by his wife and divorced her later through that same repeated character of his wife. So, no matter your differences as a couple, do not allow the crisis to continue for long, even if it concerns any quarrel in the morning or any other crisis.

83. Thinking you did not make the right choice about choosing your partner, depending on the crisis you are facing, can also make you put away your spouse. *The*

point is that both right and wrong decisions have some level of marital crisis you must deal with, and there is always something you can do to overcome your differences if you agree to overcome them. So no need to divorce. Please do not allow your choices to correct you; instead, make them suitable since it could cause divorce later.

84. Anything can distract your marriage. So beware and live the best possible marriage life.

85. If you cannot tolerate your spouse from the beginning of the marriage to when crises are moderated or solved. You cannot also tend to keep the marriage for fifty years to come, and you need to be able to keep your marriage for the next

fifty years to mean that you can be a divorcee on your next anniversary.

Remember that tolerance is very good for any marriage, not only for second marriages but also for God-given first marriages. Most couples would love to be the tolerating type in their second or third marriages rather than the first ones, and it does not sound like that since it is a total stupidity to be tolerating in your remarriage.

86. If you are fond of coming home late from work due to the dislike of your spouse, then it could soon destroy your marriage if you do not tend to consider it. *You have to know that you are a married woman or a man, and you need to be present among your children for them to*

know you better than going from club to club, friends to friends, family members to family members, and finally, to destroy your marriage with it.

Most wives will rush to take their children from their various schools, but they will never rush to attend to the needs of their husbands. Is that one too not sad? Dear wife, it will be wiser to attend to your first husband's needs as if he is your fifth husband; you do not want to lose for anything.

87. If you cannot be content with the husband or wife you are with, which no one even forced you to get married to, then divorce too will be knocking at your door soon since that is all that divorce needs to strike a beautiful and calm home

or marriage. *I have told you before that you should try to see the beauty in only your spouse, and it will save the marriage from divorce because having alternatives about men or women will only make you fool with your present spouse without knowing it.*

88. Another ugly thing or situation that destroys a beautiful marriage is when you despise or dislike your spouse to the extreme.

89. Your nagging attitude can destroy your home as a husband or a wife, and you must always be careful, especially in times of crisis. *I know it is women who nag, but some men too can do it better than women to the extent of divorce, so my man, stop the nagging, and you shall keep*

your marriage for life. Refrain from saying everything about everything. ***Be silent sometimes since most solutions also reside in wise silence. Dear wife, learn to shut up on most issues if that could destroy your home.***

90. Insulting your husband could unknowingly destroy your marriage if you do not stop it after reading this point. *Please, why must you, in your dream, even insult your husband who has sex with you or even have children with you? It is a shame, my dear sister. Maybe you learned it from your mother, and your mother was lucky to have married a very tolerating husband.*

That is why your father is still with your mother, but to you, it might not be so, and divorce will follow up after the last insult has been implemented if in case you marry an unwise husband like one of my friends. Avoid divorce, please, because your marriage is precious. Why is your marriage so valuable? Because not everybody gets it as you have gotten it. Remember that some people have been fasting and praying hard for years to have one. Therefore, it is priceless indeed.

91. Another thing that can destroy your shined marriage is when you willingly leave your position by divorce or separation in any marital crisis. *To save your marriage, please stay with your crisis; do not run away; your peers will speak ill behind you. I wonder if some couples leave their spouses and another person immediately occupies them. Still,*

the occupied person has not been changed from their harmful lifestyle. It means that it is not the person who is being left who is at fault but the one who left the marriage.

If you divorce because your husband is a drunkard, you will be surprised that another wonderful person who is better than you will take that spouse of yours and marry him to your disgrace. It means you cannot handle that man or even a woman with some challenges.

Do not be the one making your spouse misbehave in diverse negative ways and still divorce them due to that same negativity you are causing in the marriage. God will ask you one day on the judgment day just as He will judge all thieves and all marriage destroyers.

Chapter 2

IF YOU CAN'T BE REAL TO YOUR MASTER, YOUR HUSBAND, IN ALL THINGS TO MAINTAIN YOUR STEWARDSHIP AS A WIFE, THEN YOU WILL BE DIVORCED ON THE NEXT ANNIVERSARY, TO YOUR SURPRISE.

92. There would not be a callback or reconciliation because your husband will accuse you that you went away. *My dear wife, do not leave your husband when he needs you most. I believe most divorcees will go to heaven, especially those who were left by their spouses if only they will be faithful in other areas apart from marriage.*

93. If you cannot make room for your spouse's offenses, regrets not being treated well sometimes, the temptation to quit the marriage, and finally, to love when it is not favorable to love as a husband or wife, you can divorce, to my surprise. *You have to keep your marriage with all knowledge and not with vain gossip. Remember that there is nothing beautiful about divorce, not even the spelling of it.*

94. I do not trust that I can live in your beautiful marriage if you cannot be submissive enough to your husband as a wife. Humble yourself to your husband. It has the power to save your home.

95. As a wife, if you cannot learn to create good memories in your husband's mind

for you to be remembered in times of crisis, your husband will not see your benefit in the marriage since many husbands want some level of evidential good times from their wives. *Note that some good memories created in men's minds make them claim they love whomever they love as wives.*

96. Suppose you are fond of disobeying direct orders from your husband, especially in times of marital crisis. In that case, you will no longer stay in the marriage if you are unfortunate enough to marry a man who is highly interested in instructions being carried out by other people. *How would you feel if your little boy under ten years old disobeys your direct orders given to him?*

Will you feel stressed out, angry, disrespected, lost, and most of all, beat him? Remember that is what your husband will also think if you disobey his direct orders as a wife since you are under him by scripture. Maybe he will not feel all that I have written above, but he will feel to end the marriage upon your inability to take direct orders from him.

97. Most couples start their marriages so well, but along the way, they change to be negative as the marriage grows into other anniversaries. *Unfortunately, that is where divorce is also interested in striking to destroy the home. So won't it be appropriate to maintain the excellent husband or wife you are since people are desperately wicked, and your spouse could be one of them without knowing it*

yourself, in that he or she will not consider reconciliation in case the marriage is partially broken?

98. This also breaks down marriages quickly, which is if you turn out to be greater, glorious, accepted, wealthier, known, and lovely than your master, who is your spouse. If you use those opportunities to abuse your husband or wife in the marriage, then divorce will surely follow within the shortest time, too. *However, the solution to these challenges is to put those opportunities behind you and esteem your spouse more than those material things. Your marriage will be stable, especially in times of marital crisis.*

99. If you fail to honor your marriage and your spouse from time to time as the marriage grows, you will also lose that marriage and that spouse with time since no one can be with something for long if they do not genuinely respect such a person.

100. As a husband or a wife, you must prepare for the surprises that will come with your spouse in the future to avoid divorce. Marital crises in the form of surprises have been one of the channels through which many divorces have been implemented. I do not want you to be part of that, especially if you are a religious person. *Anything that comes as a surprise can easily break down your marriage, and you must be careful as you go on your marital journey.*

101. If you are not extremely careful, there might be a thousand and one ugly things that could destroy your beautiful marriage, and three of them are Facebook, apps, and many other internet accesses. Many married couples have another rival beside them, but they do not know it.

Internet access has made most married couples lose their time with their partners. The truth is that constant time spent on mobile phones can take all of the emotions you have to give to your spouse and that actions in the marriage can reduce your sexual activeness or affection and can also make your marriage boring, that is, if you become addicted to it and the marriage will finally be broken upon that if it is not intervened on time.

I am not saying you should not use your smartphone; you can give less time to it and use a more significant portion of your time to build relationships with your husband or wife and even your children.

102. Being irresponsible always as a husband to your children's daily affairs, such as providing the food and clothes and where your family will put their heads, will make your wife think that she has made a big mistake by marrying you, and the marriage will be broken upon that. My dear husband, your primary duty in the marriage is to fight harder to bring daily bread to your family's table.

Make your wife proud of you. Being proud of yourself is a way of always defending yourself when the need arises, and that will keep the marriage going for life without divorce. Remember that women love husbands who are responsible for their daily duties, especially regarding food.

103. Secretly and openly abusing your wife will make her run away one day, and that will lead to divorce by the end of the day. Therefore, if I were you, I would always quit the temptation that will tell me to beat my wife no matter how she pushes me to the wall. Remember this and try to do it; if your wife pushes you to the wall, try to pass through the wall rather than turning back to hit her because wives can be helpful most of the time. Still, they can also be troublesome sometimes, too. I believe you know that, so beware of them

and do not put yourself into trouble through them, especially your wife.

104. Having too many friends to the dislike of your spouse can destroy your marriage in the future.

105. Another ugly thing that can destroy your home and marriage immediately after you get into marriage is to allow other people to send you souvenirs of love. Know that most husbands are jealous. If you do not take care of yourself, your husband will sharply send you away from the marriage because your spouse will feel he is being shared with another person all this while. Also, the tendency of jealousy will turn to tension later, leading to another ugly thing in the marriage and finally the divorce,

especially when you mostly need yourselves couples.

If you are a married wife or a husband, know how and when to get some gifts from the opposite sex because there are significant temptations with that leading to ugly divorce or even separation.

106. Some people are misers; no wonder they lose their loved ones. Note that the world loves givers, so if you do not turn to give to your family and that of your husband or wife, he or she will not love to be with you anymore, no matter how long you have been together with yourselves. One day will be a bad day for you if you do not throw away the attitude of being a miser or someone who does not give alms.

107. Suppose you allow your loved ones to intrude into your marriage affairs without knowing your other partner. In that case, I tell you the truth: your marriage can be broken soon since many married people want their marriage to be in silence. So tame your parents, sisters, and well-wishers so they can give maximum respect to your husband or wife and establish the marriage.

I remember a confident wife who allowed his biological brother to lock up his husband in prison due to some marital issues. How can that marriage continue if the man cannot genuinely forgive by divine order? A particular husband too allowed his sister to insult his beautiful wife about her private parts, which led to divorce finally. Why should this be so? The fact is that any man who allows his wife to be vulnerable is a weak husband and deserves not to be called a husband in the first place.

I believe the final letter in the spellings of a husband is "D," which means to defend your wife for your entire life on earth. Are you a weak husband? Do you assert your weak wife in the presence of your family, especially in times of crisis? If you do not, then divorce will surely be your portion soon, whether you like it or not. Do you have a sister or brother who has intruded into your marriage for some time now to disturb your marital peace? Note that that sister or brother of yours will see you as a fool after your marriage has been broken down since you allowed your spouse to be vulnerable before them.

108. Imbalance in childbirth can also destroy your marriage without knowing it yourself. One thing you must know is that most couples are just looking for a child, and you have gotten only female or male, and you are complaining about it. Forget about having balance in your children. Instead, search for how beautifully you can raise your children to be responsible children in your community since most couples have gotten the balance in the children they want.

Still, they are not doing any better things for them to be great in the future. If you are too worried about getting a gender balance in your children, remember that there are more great people than you, but yet they do not have a gender balance in their children, and they are cool with it.

109. If you cannot bear the mistakes of your spouse, then you could also divorce.

110. Another severe thing that can destroy your marriage in the future is when you disagree with the Word of God that you have been made one by marriage through the exact word of God. Nothing (money, fame, unfaithfulness, and other challenges) should break your beautiful union down, especially in times of marital crisis.

I believe by the word of God that we have even been made one by marriage than our mothers who gave birth to us, so your spouse needs to be respected just as you respect your parent and do not make your husband or wife look stupid in the presence of your parent since you would also not like that if he or she does that to you.

111. Secretly following another rich woman or man can damage your home if you are caught one day. Please do not be greedy, my friend, husband, or wife. Anytime you are tempted to destroy your marriage because of coming across rich people in life, remember that what it will profit a man if he gets the world and loses his soul (marriage).

And that word should alert you to be stable in your marriage since divorce is not good to be practiced among the children of men. **After all, is righteousness not better than silver and gold?** Your godly marriage is more glorious than the money you will chase after from the other wealthy men and women out there than your present spouse. Be content with your spouse, lest you fall into earthly temptations that could make you empty or a divorcee later.

112. If you refuse to come back once again into marriage after having some number of separation challenges, you shall secretly end the last one with a legal divorce. Do not say that after this or that separation, you will no longer go back into marriage again. If you are having multiple separations, it simply means that you have not yet gotten the best solution,

and you need not give up on yourselves, too.

Take this from me: separation does not come to couples to end the marriage but rather to allow them to make the necessary corrections to what separated them and continue the marriage once again to the glory of God, especially if both couples are Christians or any other religious bodies who believe in the Most High God.

I wonder if most couples do not want their children to be separated from each other, but they are separated themselves or almost to be separated. It is not possible because the moment you get yourself separated as a married couple, your children too will be separated soon, and it is just a matter of time and who wants to possess the children after the divorce or separation.

113. If you think you cannot take the lying nature of your spouse, then you shall also divorce pretty soon because the vast world is lying in all manner of lies we cannot comprehend. I see the prophets and the apostles telling all levels of lies behind their pulpits; how much more are the church members? One thing you must know is that your spouse was far involved in various types of lies before you met yourselves, and you expect such a spouse to stop telling lies because you are married to each other; you are a joker who is searching for the truth to be said at all times.

If you catch your spouse telling lies right to your face, please allow him or her to confess to God and you, but do not use that opportunity to divorce your husband or wife. **(It could be any form of lies at all, such as she told you she was a virgin, but when you went into her, she was not closer to it all, and many other ones I do not want to talk about).** If you take it cool when you are told a lie, it is an excellent sign of having much knowledge about human nature yourself.

But if you divorce upon all this advice, you will still take another liar in the future if you attempt another marriage. But let me ask you: don't you tell lies to make your business successful, win some contracts, and get many more benefits in life? Call me and tell me you do not tell lies, and I will know that you are the main problem leading your marriage into a state of divorce.

114. Not improving yourself as a husband in any angle of life will make you run away from the marriage yourself. The fact is, because of the ego in you, you cannot stand it if your wife is being promoted here and there because she is doing her best to climb to the top of perfection, and you cannot also stand it if your spouse is practicing righteousness whiles you are swimming in your sin both inside and outside the marriage.

That will tempt you to run away in the shortest time, so it will be proper to work on yourself to be optimistic about what your spouse positively is and avoid harmful lifestyles since it is not even good in the first place.

Because light and darkness cannot be in one place, by all means, the darkness will run away, leaving the light to suffer the consequences of loneliness alone though married.

115. Another great thing or obstacle that can destroy your home and marriage in the future is allowing your spouse to go through their challenges alone. Why did you marry in the first place, then? My brother or sister, you have to know that because of the difficulties of this world, God made everything in two.

One, to comfort one another, and two, to give advice since two heads are always better than one, as the Bible says. Most couples want to still be in marriage with their spouses after they have betrayed them. How possible will that be? Do not leave your spouse alone in their critical times, but show that you seriously care, that you care but just that you cannot cure, and that your spouse is part of your flesh according to the word of God.

How can you leave one of your fleshes at other places you do not even care about and still want to enjoy what you abandoned when you were needed most? Divorce will come if your spouse is not the very considerate type.

116. Another severe thing that can destroy your marriage later or sooner is when you choose not to take anything good from all

that I have written so far in this volume of the book.

Remember that knowledge is compelling, and when one has it, they have it all in all, and it could save their marriage and home someday compared to when one does not. However, if you do not know how to read, you must listen to marital advice because it will also save your marriage in times of marital crisis apart from reading it yourself.

117. As an anti-divorce activist and a pastor, I pray for you that you do not divorce today or even in the future simply because I believe all marital crises can be solved through proper handling of knowledge, prayers, and also if only you can allow yourself to tolerate, to be

wronged most often, to be talked to. Most of all, listen to the one who will call you for the continuation of the marriage, especially in times of marital crisis.

Please expect more of the ugly things that could destroy your beautiful marriage in volume two of this book, which will be coming soon. Please, my dear husband or wife friend, I pray you do not read this book alone; it will be great to allow your spouse to also look through it so that he or she has an equal balance of the knowledge you have since you are not in your marriage alone but with your spouse.

Note that you can be knowledgeable about divorce and marital crisis handling, but if your spouse does not have the same knowledge, then the divorce will be implemented from that side of the lack of knowledge. That is why I want you to involve your spouse in your readings.

118. Any wife whose birth delay gave birth to beautiful and wondrous babies. Hannah gave birth to Samuel, the well-known prophet in the Bible. Elizabeth gave birth to John the Baptist, who made way for Jesus Christ. Sarah gave birth to Isaac, and Rebecca gave birth to the twins Esau and Jacob after 20 years of delay in conceiving. Jacob gave birth to Joseph and Benjamin, Jacob's choicest. Manoah – gave birth to Sampson, the most muscular man in the Bible.

119. Marriage alone cannot make one stop fornication but rather a marriage with

solid self-discipline, not grace or the absorbance of the word of God.

120. Divorce can sometimes be suitable for some couples, but it can never lessen the consequences that come with it.

121. If love fades, dangerous things follow up. So maintain yours.

122. Until you get a partner in crime, you could indeed be on the edge of divorce one day if you are not fortunate. Partners in crime cover up one's weaknesses and will not let go of you quickly, even if the situation demands it.

123. Sometimes, you fall into ugly situations that you do not like but are cool

because other people will learn from them.

124. You cannot easily teach your spouse what they could not learn in the multiple years before meeting you. So be cool, dear teacher.

125. Someone will always be there to show you more love and attention than your spouse does, and that could happen in your second marriage if you divorce due to that deception.

126. What you can bear, endure, and overcome in your marriage can sustain your home, but not what you enjoy today.

127. The sweet aroma of a mother's love can never be compared to the

compassionate affection of a good wife. A mother could have alternatives for children, but a wife would love to grow old with her first husband without divorce.

128. When someone dies, never say they are going to hell or heaven, for no one knows the state that a person dies in, righteously or un-righteously, irrespective of the person's status before dying. That should not even be your husband or wife. Leave judgment to God

129. When people find God for you, it becomes too expensive to buy him, but seeing him yourself makes it cheap.

130. If you do not know how expensive your spouse is, you will easily let go of them ignorantly.

131. In life, you will be accused and be accused again, but overcoming seven accusations could be the beginning of your greatness. Nothing comes for free.

132. If you are fond of using sharp language toward your spouse, it could lead to divorce later.

133. Being overly spiritual can also destroy your home. Over spirituality has destroyed many homes, and you can be next if you do not learn to balance your marriage and ministry. This is one of the many reasons many pastors' marriages break down—imbalance in marriage.

134. Both known and unknown accusations have destroyed many beautiful homes and marriages, and yours could be part of it if you accuse your spouse of something or nothing.

135. A knife in your kitchen can destroy your beautiful home because one partner might think the other spouse will hurt them with it if there is a pending problem.

136. Lateness from church can also bring down the beauty of your marriage if you do not know how to manage both your church and home.

137. Failure in the aspect of your spouse could make you abandon them. So, strengthen your commitment to all things.

138. Too much complaining can surprisingly destroy your home and marriage.

139. Hiding your income or money from your spouse can finally put away your spouse in a vanishing mode. If your husband or wife is open to you about their incomes, why hide yours from them?

140. Always wanting your spouse to be the helping type to you will disappoint you, which could push you out of the marriage.

141. Sometimes, disallowing your spouse to go out with you, especially when the marriage has been over ten years, will make your spouse think you have

abandoned them. It's always good to revive your love since love quenches sometimes.

142. Your church, too, can destroy your home and marriage, that is if your spouse does not like that church of yours. So, always come to understand your religious lives.

143. If you are fond of praying for your spouse or marriage from time to time, the devil can peep through to destroy it.

144. If you do not support your spouse in prayer in their predicament, they will think you do not care, which could destroy your home and marriage.

145. Listening to your sisters and brothers who had divorced their husbands and wives will surely make you divorce in marital crises. Many people divorce because they see others do the same. It is not healthy. Heal your home with their experience rather.

146. Getting tired of your spouse's crisis will surely make you put away your spouse, and that will not make you look for corrections instead.

147. Visiting your mother most often but still married will make your wife think that you have not entirely separated from her, and she can quickly feel that you should go and be with your mother instead of her.

148. Refusing to see your spouse as your spouse in marital crises will indeed cause you to abandon your marriage.

149. Being unable to defend your husband as a wife will make you dishonor him, possibly leading to divorce.

150. The inability to regulate the cold or hot in your room will damage your relationship with your spouse. Remember that anything can destroy your beautiful home and marriage.

151. Solemnly mispleading your spouse for your means will make your spouse cold, costing you your beautiful home and marriage.

152. Your spouse always forces you to make love to you when you do not want it. It will make you think that your spouse is filled with the devil, and that can also destroy your growing marriage.

153. Dragging your children with your spouse right in the marriage can make you go away with yourselves to keep your children personally instead of you both keeping them as a couple

154. Forgetting that you are married alone can make you abandon your marriage because forgetfulness is dangerous.

155. If you do not satisfy your spouse sexually and the complaint begins to rise, it will make your spouse cheat, and that could destroy the marriage later on.

156. Having the mindset that your second marriage will be more glamorous than this present one will slowly or quickly make you abandon your present spouse for the fantasy you have been having.

157. To your surprise, your inability to maintain yourself or love will cause your divorce.

158. There are more than a thousand ugly things that could destroy a beautiful marriage, and one of them is having an attitude of annoying your spouse through your lifestyle, which will cause the marriage to break down.

159. Another thing that could destroy your home and the relationship you have

with your spouse is pornographic content. Pornography is purely a work of act, and most of the actors and actresses take medications to prolong their ejaculations. So having the attitude of watching porn as a couple will make to be expecting the same acts from your spouse, which may be a mirage to you.

160. Longing to destroy your marriage yourself will surely make it very easy for you to destroy it compared to when someone else wants to destroy it for you. Unfortunately, most divorces go through the way of marriage.

161. Not understanding the meaning of your spouse's crisis will make you put it away before you know it later.

152. It would help if you saw your spouse's immediate importance in making you abandon your home. Remember that one's importance cannot purely be identified when such a person is there with you.

163. Losing the focus as a married man or woman will make you fool sooner, which will undoubtedly lead to other harmful incidents, and the final one will be divorce.

164. If you do not cherish your spouse's profession, you will leave soon, simply because we will all live with our spouse's career for a very long time. *Esteem your* lucrative or small careers, and learn to better yourselves as couples.

165. Allowing your temperament to guide you roughly will lead you to divorce if your spouse does not understand your temperament.

166. Trusting yourself or your spouse too much can lead to divorce, as humans are unreliable, and your spouse is one of them.

167. If you cherish your boss more than your spouse, your relationship with your spouse will break down.

168. Anything could break down our marriages, and we must always be careful to make them successful. One ugly thing is marital tiredness, which can make you leave the marriage sooner or later. You have to know that marriage is the center for fulfilling responsibilities, and by all

means, one will be tired because you are a human being, for that matter. It would help if you regulated your stress to sustain the marriage if it seems shaken.

169. Having a waxed mind about your spouse will never allow the marriage to stand. Do not be headstrong about your spouse.

170. Extremely disrespecting your spouse will surely break down the marriage in the future if he lacks patience. Remember that you must respect your husband before any marriage you enter into works, and it'll be better for you to keep your first spouse as a wife.

171. Pastors have been one of the sources through which quick divorces come, and you must not be a victim. Most pastors are

sleeping with people's wives and do not need to be in that church if you *reverence* your marriage, less you be the next victim to your liken.

172. Marriage should not be carnal; you need to be spiritual to see the things beyond you lest divorce follows.

173. Your spouse seeing you ending your life could make them abandon you with divorce since many people do not naturally want to hear or see failure.

174. If you fail to work in a team with your spouse in marriage, it could tempt one of you to depart in shame, which will affect both of you in the future marriage. A teamwork partner will not be me but us. It is just like a pilot and his co-pilot; both

of them are important in case a crisis occurs in the plane.

175. If you do not want to divorce as a couple, attack the conflicts instead of your spouse. Please do not hold your spouse on.

176. Another thing that could destroy your home and marriage is turning to a roommate instead of a marriage mate. Do not see your husband or wife as your sibling lest you know another person as your sex mate.

177. As a couple, a lack of serious commitment among you will destroy your beautiful home and marriage. A committed spouse sees their marriage as for life, even during marital crises. One

needs to honor one's partner to maintain the marriage. If you are too committed, you shall not use words such as 'we are a mistake to each other, let us cease the relationship by divorce, and if it's you, then I will not marry anyone again after our divorce.'

178. Your mother being a witch could make you leave your marriage because most witches do not allow good things to happen. This is why you must not abandon prayer as you approach other unknown anniversaries.

179. You not understanding spiritual things yourselves also makes you divorce to your shame.

180. How wrongly you start your beautiful marriage can also bring it down if you do not change your beginning errors as you grow as a couple.

181. Not containing your spouse's quick changes can make you look down on your spouse, which could cause you extreme sadness during a divorce.

182. One day, your spouse will stop going to church as usual and will start to go to the mosque or even to be a fetish priest; if you do not love your spouse beyond something, you shall indeed let go of your spouse for a religious purpose. Note that marriage and love must go beyond a spiritual standard.

183. Your children's attitudes alone can make you destroy your marriage. Some of your children could become stubborn to the extent of chasing your husband or wife from the marriage. Therefore, you must also learn how to tame your children as a spouse.

184. If you are fond of condemning your spouse, your spouse will no longer love to be in the marriage with you.

185. If you do not know how to live well with your in-laws, some of them convince your spouse to leave the marriage soon. In-laws can make the marriage to be uncomfortable, especially for uncommitted spouses.

186. Why must you leave your marriage at all? Remember that if you leave your home, another person will take your spouse and deal with the crisis you were unable to, and maybe you will also go in for another imperfect spouse, which we have been doing since ancient times.

187. If you do not tend to listen to god in times of marital crises, it will make you divorce the marriage you do not have to leave.

188. If you are too much in the flesh, too, you will not understand the spiritual needs of your marriage. Life is not only physical; remember this always. Seek God

189. The fact is that some things will never change about your spouse, whether

you like it or not, and forcing those things to be changed will push you out of the marriage because you do not know that only god can change people.

190. If you are too curious about life and your marriage, that same curiosity can lead to divorce. Some couples even think they will divorce and know how it feels, but what sort of curiosity is that?

Chapter 3

JOINING THE OCCULT TO THE DISPLEASURE OF YOUR SPOUSE WILL SURELY MAKE YOU DIVORCE ONE DAY BECAUSE MOST OCCULTISTS

They do not want their secrets exposed, so they will prefer that you leave your spouse to marry a spouse from their midst.

191. Always thinking that divorce could be the best option to end the crisis will also make you leave the marriage, and that will cost you because divorce is never the best, though it might seem so.

192. Not knowing how to cook could destroy your home. Most men or husbands want delicious food, but you cannot. Take your time to learn how to cook.

193. Note that everybody loves good things. If you are good at telling your spouse you love them as often as possible. I bet another person would do that for you. In addition, do you know what happens when telling someone you love them?

194. If you cannot exercise reason or thinking capabilities, you could divorce yourselves as a couple.

195. The top secret things only your spouse knows about you can make them ignorantly divorce you. How do you tell

your spouse some of your dirty deals since not everyone has the strong heart to stand up to life's pressures?

196. Another ugly thing that could destroy your home and marriage is greediness. Greediness is wanting more but not having enough. Greediness has put many good spouses in prison and ended most of them in divorce. Be content, my friend and dear wife; do not push your husband to the wall to commit greed.

197. This is very important; if you do not have often sex with your spouse, it will prompt your spouse to sin, and divorce could follow.

198. Husband, you do not tend to reason together on issues with your spouse; it

will tell her that you are in the marriage with yourself and could make her run away to go in for the type which includes his wife in marital affairs since a successful is usually based on communication and often agreement.

199. If you disagree with your husband on the school and future of your children, it will make him leave the marriage since that shows you do not respect him as a wife.

200. Allowing your pastor to be esteemed more than your husband will cause your husband to be jealous. I hope you know about jealousy among men.

201. If *you esteem* your church more than your wife, you will lose your marriage. So, be always balanced as a husband.

202. Neglecting the Holy Spirit will cause you to lose your esteem for your spouse, which, unfortunately, leads to divorce. Many Christians are divorcing because the Holy Spirit is no longer in them. If the Holy Spirit is with you, you will be patient in times of marital crisis.

203. Cooking and washing for your husband are valuable in the stability of marriages. So, being unable to cook for your family as a wife will push your husband outside the marriage, which could destroy your home and marriage if he is the type who loves to eat a wife's delicacies. Some husbands do not have

problems with this like me, but if your husband wants you to serve him, my dear, do it. Put pride and foolishness down and help your husband.

204. Attracting some serious and unserious sexually transmitted infections will disallow your spouse to sleep with you as a couple, and that can be the basis of your division. Be careful of the women you put your penis into them and the people you allow to touch you as a woman.

205. Your inability to adjust because your spouse has changed negatively will tempt you to think that divorce should be the best solution, and you will realize you have implemented a quick divorce to your dislike.

206. An extreme lust towards other people but not your spouse could also happen to destroy your beautiful marriage.

207. Being unable to control your jealousy as a spouse will eventually cause you to hurt your sweet spouse, which could also end the marriage.

208. Because you do not know the type of spouse you got married to, you need to be very careful since you do not see the crisis that will tear you apart. Do not drag minor issues for them to turn into dragons you cannot handle again, which are common causes of divorce.

209. If you are a problematic spouse, I tell you that you cannot find most marital

solutions. So be soft since you cannot be stronger than the consequences of divorce.

210. Anything could break down our marriages, and one of them is allowing your job to take control of your senses. Your marital home should be a home, not a working place.

211. Sometimes, marital crises are like taking stripes at your back; the weaker you look, the more the pain will be. Therefore, it would help if you were strong mentally to face your daily marital crisis to save your marriage from divorce.

212. There was a wife who had been complaining about her husband's smoking nature; one day, as they were having a

walk, the rain started, and they got wet and cold. To the husband's surprise, the wife started searching for the lighter the husband used to smoke firewood to light some firewood. This means there could be something good in your spouse, even though you may not like their predicament or character.

213. If you cannot wait for your spouse after they have been imprisoned for a long or short time, you are divorced for a long time. Note that marriage can continue after imprisonment if both sides have genuine love. I will quickly return to my wife after she returns from prison.

214. Getting into sexual contact with another person or woman can easily make your wife go away since you do not know

whether your spouse is just looking for that opportunity to unleash that. Therefore, would it not be wiser to avoid strange women in your life since they will by means come one way or another

215. My dear wife, if you become very stubborn with your husband, he will let you go out for a marital break, ending the marriage.

216. Do not forget that some ugly things could happen after thirty years of marriage, and one of them is deception: thinking that you have it all.

217. If you think you are the man so no woman can control you, then you cannot be in marriage because most of our wives are mothers, and do mothers do

sometimes? They control. Remember that the bible says that man does not have power over the body.

218. Sending a wrong text message to your spouse, which is supposed to be sent to your boy or girlfriend, can slowly lead to contention and divorce.

219. Refusing to pursue your spouse when a separation occurs will permanently end your marriage. As for separation, it must come, but how you deal with yourselves after that is what matters. Do not say if they have gone or she should go; it will not be healthy to stabilize your home from divorce.

220. Involving in robbery or criminal acts will quench your spouse's love for you

because no one wants to mingle with the bad. What sort of job are you into, and is it helping your marriage?

221. If you cannot give a second chance to your husbands or wife after a grave mistake has been committed, then you shall surely be on the journey of divorce simply because marriage is a long journey with difficulties.

222. If you are fond of making divorce statements to your spouse, you shall surely divorce because no one is greater than their words.

223. I know our children count little when it comes to handling our marital crisis, but if you refuse to listen to that little voice of your children on not to divorce yourselves

as a couple, then divorce shall rain. Remember that god can speak through your children.

224. If you have made a big mistake in the marriage and cannot quickly apologize, divorce can come through because perhaps that is all your spouse could be waiting for.

225. Do not be too stubborn before people or even your spouse because of a crisis. Do not cry secretly in your room because it will indeed prevent the marriage from continuing. If the crisis comes, be humble and deal with it; the right solution will come.

226. Another ugly thing that could destroy your home is you not considering the ugly

state that your children will be in if you put yourselves away as couples. You will surely break down the marriage in times of marital crisis. Remember never to put yourselves first in marital crises but in your children's warfare.

227. If you are fond of fighting over things money can buy, you shall surely divorce because money should solve your marital crisis when you have some.

228. If you are also found fighting over things money cannot buy, you shall surely divorce in times of marital crisis. Money can buy cars, houses, beds, sofa chairs, and many more, and some of the things that money cannot buy are love, understanding, peace, affection, and, most of all, genuine and godly marriage.

229. As a husband, if you do not take it as a habit to pay the daily bills that come with the marriage, you could leave for that reason.

230. I tell you the truth that if you are not able to accommodate your marital nonsense, you will divorce in the future because nonsense is complicated to overcome if one is not conscious of it.

231. I was taught to believe that some divorces result from curses; if that were true, then you might be working on those curses as a couple, making you divorce just as your parents divorced. Remember, you must be different from yourself because you have seen the light. Note that curses are instituted through our lifestyles,

mistakes, and how we deal with ourselves as a couple.

232. The attitude of I do not care reigning in your marriage could also break down your marriage if you do not change.

233. If you do not listen to your husband most often, he will please you and leave the marriage for someone better than you to take your place as you go.

234. If you do not work to support your husband in all things, he will love to let you go away from the marriage, and another person will occupy your dirty place.

235. I have said and am saying again that regretting your marriage will make it to

put away your spouse. Please note that you regret your part of us, especially if things are not going well with us. I regretted getting into some businesses at the beginning of my life, but I am glad today that I did not close down those businesses when challenges came around. That is what your marriage and family should also be.

236. One ugly thing that could destroy your home and marriage is when you think that the money, time, and energy you used to marry is reverence less; for that matter, you can remarry because you still have those same virtues. Even if those virtues are still there, remember that you must overcome your marriage crisis to save the marriage from divorce, my dear married couples.

237. If you cannot turn rightly to the sexual position of your spouse, divorce can come through that. And remember that turning to the sexual position of your husband demands the highest humility as a wife.

238. I know that most couples do not want to kiss their spouses; what a shame! Do you not know that it is kissing that makes sexual intercourse pleasurable? This divorce could come if your spouse loves kissing while you do not like it.

239. Being deceived by your ex can crush your relationship with your spouse. Respect the man or woman who married you; it will bless your family.

240. Being too carnal about earthly things will cause you not to honor your spouse. I wonder if some couples can ignore their spouse's existence because of money.

241. Over-valuing, over-trusting, and over-everything could also destroy your growing marriage. Remember that doing something over is very dangerous.

242. Changing your church one day could also change your marriage, as many people love their churches because they represent Christ. If you come from one church, do not allow marital crises to make you change your loved church.

243. If you do not tell your spouse your secret admirers and they find out, it

quickly tells them you are in some relationship with them.

244. Be truthful in telling your dreams, especially about people who sleep with you in your dreams, because spiritual husbands and wives can make you divorce your sweet spouse simply because the relationship you have with your spiritual spouses can be tempting.

245. If you fail to pray for marriage and that of your spouse, the evil around your environs will make you run away from marriage one day. Prayer is mighty. Therefore, do not avoid it. Even the sons of the devil make some prayers to keep things that are important to them. How much more are you that is religious? Most divorced couples you see today were once

upon a time sweet couples, but something happened, which is the negligence of prayer.

246. Dear wife, if you are good at comparing your husband to what you see outside, I bet you that divorce could be knocking on your door when you don't like it. Many wives and husbands have been possessed by their friends, and you must not be a victim.

247. Having struggled with my faith throughout, I solemnly believe that evil spirits can destroy beautiful marriages. It would help if you were careful about your spouse's character.

248. I told you in the volume of this book that there could be more than 1000 ugly

things that could destroy your beautiful marriage, and one of them is not keeping your mouth shut about the breakthroughs of your spouse. Remember, only some people are happy about your success concerning your marriage.

249. Amazingly, anything can destroy your beautiful marriage, so involving in gay activities in the later part of your marriage can also break down your marriage, and you need not be deceived into that as the world is a crucial place to be.

250. If you are fond of disturbing your wife because you have an alternative of a woman somewhere, you will abandon your spouse to divorce.

251. If you are too proud and, for that matter, you cannot turn to the sexual position of your spouse, I tell you the truth that it will make your spouse run away to chase other unimportant ones.

252. A strange friend between you and your spouse can promptly destroy your sweet marriage. So check with your new and old friends to ensure that divorce is not hiding in them.

253. Do not trust yourselves too much as couples, lest your marriage be broken on that same trust you have for yourselves.

254. Do you know that your work could be the source of your divorce, especially if your spouse is unhappy?

255. Impregnating your wife is not the responsibility of taking care of those children, and so if you force yourself to take care of your children, it will discourage your wife, and that could destroy your home.
256. Your close friend can make you leave the marriage for someone better than you to occupy. All you can know is that your close is lusting for your wife while you do not know. So keep your spouse's distance from your spouse.

257. Snubbing your husband could destroy your home and marriage if your spouse does not understand the crisis.

258. If you are fond of threatening your spouse with divorce statements, I tell you the truth: Your marriage could be broken.

259. If you cannot protect why you got married, those same reasons will make your divorce soon. Respect the reason your spouse used to marry you.

260. If you are not of use to your spouse, your spouse, too, is not seeing the benefits of your presence in the marriage, which could lead to divorce. So show your spouse that all of your being is in the marriage, and your spouse will respect that if they are evidential

261. Taking a loan to fulfill your marriage's obligation and being unable to pay in time will put unnecessary pressure on you, and you could be divorced from that.

262. Directly doing things your spouse hates could generate long-term contention, leading to divorce. Why must you do things that your husband or wife does not want? Are you not going to destroy your home instead of saving it?

263. Miscarriage and multiple miscarriages have broken many good marriages, and you could be part of it if you are not of food courage. Be careful to love yourselves even if you lose your ninth child if you did not marry purposely for children.

264. The lack of quick response to your spouse's urgent need could also destroy your home.

265. If you fail to introduce your spouse to people who need you to know them, insecurity will follow divorce.

266. Crises are not meant to destroy us but to work on them for perfection. However, if you fear your marital turmoil, then you shall surely divorce through them.

267. Directly insulting your in-laws can also destroy your growing marriage if you are good at controlling your tongue.

268. If you ignore your husband, you will be surprised by what he can do to you. Obey your husband always; it is the secret to overcoming many marital crises.

269. Relating badly to your in-laws can lead to divorce, to your surprise. Many

people believe that family existed before marriage.

270. A lack of compassion toward your husband or wife could result in divorce. Compassion is one of the best keys to repairing a broken relationship, so do not ignore it, especially in times of marital crisis.

271. Drinking and gambling with friends can destroy your home. Seize from such a thing if you get involved. Nowadays, there is gambling everywhere and it is making many families depressed and frustrated, leading them to a fast divorce each day.

272. Your smelling vagina, because you do not take care of it well by bathing

regularly, can also destroy your beautiful marriage. Remember that most husbands love to send their heads under or around their wives vagina. So treat yours well if your husband is good at licking your vagina to his pleasure. Do not infect your husband or wife because you do not bathe.

273. Lack of self-control can also destroy your home and marriage. The fact is that most people or couples are married because they lack self-control. However, I have identified that you must still practice some form of self-control, though you do not have self-control, lest you mess up yourselves as a couple, since many instances in marriage require you to be strong in the aspect of self-control. For example, what would you do if you had

not slept with your spouse for some reason?

274. Allowing yourself to come so low to sleep with your daughters or sons will immediately shut down your relationship with your spouse.

275. Temptations have been a significant source of broken homes. So the temptation to steal, kill, destroy, leave the marriage, separate, abuse your spouse, being cruel in different ways or acts will surely ruin your home and marriage.

276. If you are seen or fond of visiting herbalists and spiritualists, your spouse may feel ill about you, and the marriage will be broken upon that.

277. I am telling you that there are many reasons why you may not enjoy your marriage, including having too many expectations in your marriage or towards your spouse.

278. If you have it in your heart to divorce your spouse one day, it will happen because our thoughts make up our personalities.

279. If you are also indifferent to your spouse, you should divorce because a double-minded person cannot receive anything good or positive in life.

280. If you do not trust god with your crisis, you shall surely divorce because crisis sometimes makes us forget about everything.

281. One thing that could destroy your home and marriage is being greedy about everything in life. Man, be careful what you take to your possession because you cannot eat everything you are greedy about.

282. If you allowed yourself to be charmed by another woman somewhere, you shall surely divorce your present wife you took money and time to marry. Remember that wicked women in town will do anything to have you in their possession. Note also that whether you are charmed or not, you will feel the consequences alone, which could even transfer to the next generation. Anytime you have another woman apart from your wife, you could be under some deadly

spells, and your solution should be deliverance in the name of Jesus.

283. Accusing your mother of a witch could destroy your home and marriage simply because most husbands love their mothers, even if they are dragons. Therefore, wife, shut up sometimes if you do not understand your mother-in-law. If it turns out to be true that your mother-in-law is a witch, do not physically fight or insult her, send her into prayer, and never leave the marriage due to that.

284. As a husband or wife, an evil character from your side could also break down your beautiful marriage. So control yourself always and do not be mean to your spouse.

285. If you refuse to accept that marriage is full of one crisis or the other, one unknown crisis will make you run away from your blessed marriage.

286. If you do not have the thought that your wife can fall totally by one temptation, I tell you the truth that one evil temptation will make you throw away your spouse you could have instead helped than sacking. Whatever temptation you face, your face can face the same, so do not be too judgmental if one comes.

287. They are marrying someone far older than you will or can put your home into a profound silence irrespective of gender unless that spouse knows the temptation that comes with such a decision.

288. It can also destroy the marriage if you are fond of taking your husband's money without telling him. Therefore, if you have a problem with kleptomania, please deal with it before it destroys what is costly to you.

289. I remember I mistakenly replaced our padlock one day, and my wife was secretly worried about that, but I did not know. Another time, I replaced another padlock, and my wife came openly and said that I am fond of replacing padlocks. I became annoyed by the accusations, but I quickly remembered that when you are accused, you must be humbled, lest other evils follow. So you, too, if you are not able to be cool about accusations in your marriage, those same accusations will destroy your home and marriage soon.

290. Your prophet can silence your beautiful marriage simply because he has a voice, and any voice at all can break down the relationship you have with your family.

Chapter 4

I WANT TO ALERT YOU TO THE UGLY THINGS THAT COULD DESTROY YOUR HOME AND MARRIAGE.

One of them is allowing your closest friend to deceive you into letting go of your spouse.

291. If you are fond of placing your husband last or not considering him in times of severe marital crisis, it will ignorantly make you put him away.

292. Likewise, not thinking about your spouse positively, though there may be a crisis, will undoubtedly lead to divorce when you need not divorce as a couple.

293. Though they are positive adjectives, wealth, riches, honor, fame, excitement, progress, change, chance, productivity, breakthrough, and excellence can break down our marriages. That is why you must control them as you see them coming into some areas of your marriage.

294. Evil on your land could also destroy your growing marriage, and one of those evils is seeing many people around you divorcing.

295. Natural causes, too, could cause you to be divorced as a couple. One of those natural causes is your spouse being accused of something they have not done and going on to be convicted of that crime. Sometimes, you do not have control over them, so you must always be careful.

296. If you are not genuinely born again, your faithful born-again spouse could be deceived into divorce since most Christians do not understand the scriptures as they ought.

297. If it is Satan that allowed you to be put together as spouses, then that same Satan will make your divorce one day. Still, with a god-type marriage, you can easily overcome your marital crises irrespective of their weight because god is with you. Most people who overcame their marital crises in one way or another have some manner of a supreme god in them.

298. If you decide to follow the path of the devil at the later path of your marriage,

your spouse shall divorce you, and there will not be a call back because most Christians are evil. Remember that there is nothing good in the world.

299. Practicing masturbation will make you lose your sexual appetite toward your spouse, and that could push your spouse out and finally destroy the marriage.

300. If you fail to learn to grow together as a couple, one of you growing faster in anything could make you disappear in silence.

301. Leaving your husband for the woman that wants to take him away from you will make you to be a divorcee soon. My dear married couples, anyone you could marry after divorce will have the same

temptation to leave the marriage by other people. Therefore, fight harder if other partners are fighting hard to destroy your home and marriage. Do not give up easily; do not say you will leave your marriage for that new person.

302. Your extreme jealousy as a husband or wife can also make your spouse not love the marriage genuinely, which could bring up divorce.

303. If you do not have a purpose to send your marriage to the end of time, irrespective of your crisis, you shall surely end yourselves on the way, regardless of how long you have been together.

304. Not giving multiple chances to your spouse to your spouse when offenses

come will make you drop yourselves as a couple. In addition, one way to do this is to forgive easily and quickly. Remember that some crises can last long, and divorce should not be an option.

305. Your parents not agreeing to marry you at the beginning of your marriage could make one of you think that it could be why some crises are coming your way. Still, the truth is, whether your parents agree or not, there could be some crises you will think you cannot overcome.

306. Going to separate churches as couples could also destroy your growing marriage due to the different doctrines the churches teach in this dispensation. I hope it would be better to attend one church and find a better church to go to since there are

dangerous churches in town nowadays. Just agree, and do not allow religion to destroy your beautiful marriage and home.

307. Do not be a married person and still behave as if you are not married because it will portray you as someone who does not love your spouse and wishes you were divorced. Some married couples remove their wedding rings immediately after leaving their marital homes.

308. Whether we like it or not, we all have some level of weaknesses, but if your spouse does not portray one for the number of years that you have been together, don't trust them because one day it will come out, and divorce could easily

follow up if you have come across this message.

309. Your inability to tolerate yourselves as a couple will easily break your spouse or marriage, especially in marital crises, and could badly end your search for another good person. Tolerance is one of the most potent virtues all couples could ever need.

310. Involving yourself in things that your spouse will regret in the future could destroy your marriage in that same future. An example is taking an extra man or woman after your spouse and starting fights you do not want to quench quickly due to your pride. Please do not create a marital crisis by not taking good care of

your children; it could affect both your children and you in the future.

311. Rating your properties more highly than your spouse means you are a material person, which could split the marriage. You can even repeat that in your subsequent marriage if you divorce.

312. Complications that come with your wife's pregnancy can frustrate you both to leave yourselves to the chance of divorce and separation. Every marriage is affiliated with one crisis, and it is your duty as a couple to overcome yours, lest you come down to shame through divorce.

313. Suppose you do not consider how lovely you began your relationship during

marital crises. In that case, I tell you that something will make you end up with yourselves roughly on divorce, and the consequences of your actions, too, shall be terrible to your bearings. Going down memory lane will help you fight your challenges as you grow together as a couple.

314. The immediate surprises that shall come at the beginning of your marriage have the power to tear you apart if you need to be brighter. That is one of the reasons why some wonderful marriages are broken in the first one to six months.

315. Not marrying the one you truly love could bring down your marriage, especially if you do not tend to work on yourselves daily to make things right.